T0019478

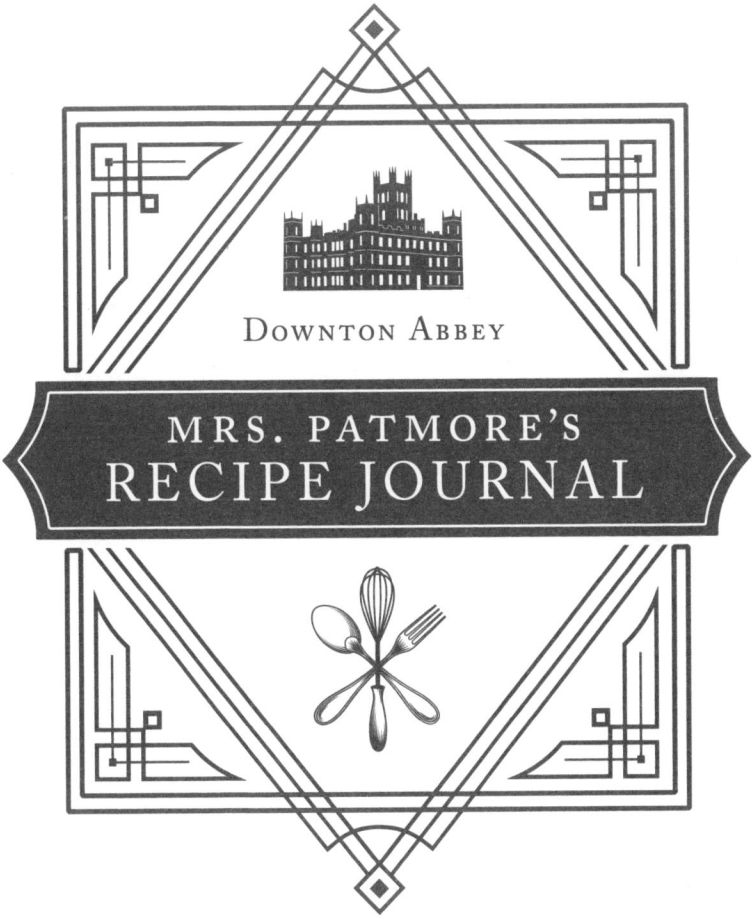
Downton Abbey
MRS. PATMORE'S
RECIPE JOURNAL

RECIPE

SERVES:

INGREDIENTS

METHOD

"Nothing in life is sure."

MRS. PATMORE

SEASON 1, EPISODE 1

RECIPE

SERVES:

INGREDIENTS

METHOD

MRS. PATMORE

There is a man who's been shaken to the roots of his soul. Everything he based his life on has proved mortal after all.

MRS. HUGHES

We've no time for philosophy, Mrs. Patmore. What can we do to help?

MRS. PATMORE

Let's send up some coffee.

SEASON 6, EPISODE 5

RECIPE

SERVES:

INGREDIENTS

METHOD

"Oh why not just serve 'em bread and cheese then and have done with it?"

MRS. PATMORE

SEASON 3, EPISODE 6

RECIPE

SERVES:

INGREDIENTS

METHOD

"There's nothing wrong with a man who can cook.
Some say the best cooks in the world are men."

MRS. PATMORE

SEASON 3, EPISODE 7

RECIPE

SERVES:

INGREDIENTS

METHOD

"It's wonderful what fear can do to the human spirit."

MRS. PATMORE

SEASON 2, EPISODE 8

RECIPE

SERVES:

INGREDIENTS

METHOD

MRS. PATMORE

I've got tea for all of us, and a snack for you later on.

MASON

You're an angel of mercy.

SEASON 6, EPISODE 5

RECIPE

SERVES:

INGREDIENTS

METHOD

"A bad workman always blames his tools."

MRS. PATMORE

SEASON 3, EPISODE 2

RECIPE

SERVES:

INGREDIENTS

METHOD

"He's very kind, you know. We should always be polite to people who are kind. There's not much of it about!"

MRS. PATMORE

SEASON 5, EPISODE 6

RECIPE

SERVES:

INGREDIENTS

METHOD

"Well, the cat's away, so we mice might as well play a little."

MRS. PATMORE

SEASON 5, EPISODE 9

RECIPE

SERVES:

INGREDIENTS

METHOD

TUFTON

But taking orders from a husband has got to be better than taking them from some jumped up lord or lady.

MRS. PATMORE

Hmm. It's still orders, isn't it?

SEASON 3, EPISODE 9

RECIPE

SERVES:

INGREDIENTS

METHOD

"Oh, well, of course, as we all know, anyone can cook."

MRS. PATMORE

SEASON 6, EPISODE 5

RECIPE

SERVES:

INGREDIENTS

METHOD

"It's that bloomin' Daisy! I've said she'll be the death of me, and now my word's come true!"

MRS. PATMORE

SEASON 1, EPISODE 5

RECIPE

SERVES:

INGREDIENTS

METHOD

"No, don't stop stirring, the bottom will burn!"

MRS. PATMORE

SEASON 2, EPISODE 4

RECIPE

SERVES:

INGREDIENTS

METHOD

DAISY

I was only trying to help.

MRS. PATMORE

Oh like Judas was only "trying to help," I s'pose, when he brought the Roman soldiers to the garden!

SEASON 1, EPISODE 5

RECIPE

SERVES:

INGREDIENTS

METHOD

"Be off with you, you cheeky devil. Go on!"

MRS. PATMORE

SEASON 3, EPISODE 9

RECIPE

SERVES:

INGREDIENTS

METHOD

"I know the popular fantasy is that you can feed six strong men from a single seed cake, but you and I know better."

MRS. PATMORE

SEASON 2, EPISODE 3

RECIPE

SERVES:

INGREDIENTS

METHOD

"Never mind that. At times like these, we must all pull together."

MRS. PATMORE

SEASON 2, EPISODE 8

RECIPE

SERVES:

INGREDIENTS

METHOD

DAISY

A penny for your thoughts.

MRS. PATMORE

They're worth a great deal more than that, thank you very much.

SEASON 2, EPISODE 2

RECIPE

SERVES:

INGREDIENTS

METHOD

"Now, what else can I give you? Another cup of tea, why not?"

MRS. PATMORE

SEASON 6, EPISODE 5

RECIPE

SERVES:

INGREDIENTS

METHOD

"Ooh talk about making a silk purse out of a sow's ear.
I wish we had a sow's ear. It'd be better than this brisket."

MRS. PATMORE

SEASON 2, EPISODE 7

RECIPE

SERVES:

INGREDIENTS

METHOD

"Daisy? Did you hear me call? Or have you gone selectively deaf?"

MRS. PATMORE

SEASON 1, EPISODE 2

RECIPE

SERVES:

INGREDIENTS

METHOD

SYBIL

Do you think it's ready?

MRS. PATMORE

I know it's ready.

SEASON 2, EPISODE 1

RECIPE

SERVES:

INGREDIENTS

METHOD

"Oh my, my, will wonders never cease?"

MRS. PATMORE

SEASON I, EPISODE I

RECIPE

SERVES:

INGREDIENTS

METHOD

"Oh, I'll have no swear words in here, thank you very much. Unless I'm doing the swearing."

MRS. PATMORE

SEASON 4, EPISODE 3

RECIPE

SERVES:

INGREDIENTS

METHOD

"What's this? Do I hear my name taken in vain?"

MRS. PATMORE

SEASON 3, EPISODE 9

RECIPE

SERVES:

INGREDIENTS

METHOD

MRS. PATMORE

But you can't manage a broth, Miss Denker, special or otherwise?

DENKER

Well, of course I would be very good at it -

MRS. PATMORE

If you only knew where to start.

SEASON 5, EPISODE 9

RECIPE

SERVES:

INGREDIENTS

METHOD

"Oh! You couldn't be harder on those potatoes if you wanted them to confess to spying."

MRS. PATMORE

SEASON 6, EPISODE 4

RECIPE

SERVES:

INGREDIENTS

METHOD

"Use an alarm clock to remind you when to put things in the oven and when to take them out."

MRS. PATMORE

SEASON 3, EPISODE 6

RECIPE

SERVES:

INGREDIENTS

METHOD

"Fold it in, don't slap it! You're making a cake, not beating a carpet!"

MRS. PATMORE

SEASON 2, EPISODE 2

RECIPE

SERVES:

INGREDIENTS

METHOD

DAISY

It's a mixer. It beats eggs and whips cream and all sorts.

MRS. PATMORE

But you and Ivy do that.

DAISY

And we'd be glad not to, thank you very much.

SEASON 4, EPISODE 1

RECIPE

SERVES:

INGREDIENTS

METHOD

"If it's all right with you,
I've to tackle tonight's dinner."

MRS. PATMORE

SEASON 5, EPISODE 1

RECIPE

SERVES:

INGREDIENTS

METHOD

"Listen to me! And get those kidneys up to the servery before I knock you down and serve your brains as fritters."

MRS. PATMORE

SEASON 1, EPISODE 2

RECIPE

SERVES:

INGREDIENTS

METHOD

"Yes. Well. Sympathy butters no parsnips. I'd better get on."

MRS. PATMORE

SEASON 5, EPISODE 3

RECIPE

SERVES:

INGREDIENTS

METHOD

THOMAS

I'm just trying to be helpful.

MRS. PATMORE

I'm afraid 'being helpful' is not something we associate you with.

SEASON 2, EPISODE 8

RECIPE

SERVES:

INGREDIENTS

METHOD

"This stuff is thirsty work."

MRS. PATMORE

SEASON 2, EPISODE 9

RECIPE

SERVES:

INGREDIENTS

METHOD

"There's lobster rissoles in Mousseline sauce or Calvados-glazed duckling, or do you fancy a little asparagus salad with Champagne-saffron vinaigrette?"

MRS. PATMORE

SEASON 3, EPISODE 3

RECIPE

SERVES:

INGREDIENTS

METHOD

"I had to get out of that kitchen if I'm not to be found dead under the table."

MRS. PATMORE

SEASON 2, EPISODE 4

RECIPE

SERVES:

INGREDIENTS

METHOD

MRS. PATMORE

I know it's cheating but I think I might get a jar of horseradish. It really isn't bad now.

DAISY

That's not like you.

SEASON 6, EPISODE 2

RECIPE

SERVES:

INGREDIENTS

METHOD

"Anyone who has the use of their limbs can make a salmon mousse."

MRS. PATMORE

SEASON 3, EPISODE 6

RECIPE

SERVES:

INGREDIENTS

METHOD

"Now steady. Even the most experienced cook can burn themself if they're not careful."

MRS. PATMORE

SEASON 2, EPISODE 1

RECIPE

SERVES:

INGREDIENTS

METHOD

"Oh I'm not just a pretty face."

MRS. PATMORE

SEASON 3, EPISODE 9

RECIPE

SERVES:

INGREDIENTS

METHOD

DAISY

I was just thinking.

MRS. PATMORE

Blimey. Batten down the hatches.

SEASON 1, EPISODE 6

RECIPE

SERVES:

INGREDIENTS

METHOD

"Now go and grate that suet before I grow old and die."

MRS. PATMORE

SEASON 2, EPISODE 3

RECIPE

SERVES:

INGREDIENTS

METHOD

"Nothing's as changeable as a young man's heart.
Take hope and a warning from that."

MRS. PATMORE

SEASON 4, EPISODE 2

RECIPE

SERVES:

INGREDIENTS

METHOD

"Have a bit of the tart if you like."

MRS. PATMORE

SEASON 3, EPISODE 9

RECIPE

SERVES:

INGREDIENTS

METHOD

MRS. PATMORE

I'm not saying poison them. Just make sure they don't find her food all that agreeable.

DAISY

By poisoning it?

SEASON 1, EPISODE 7

RECIPE

SERVES:

INGREDIENTS

METHOD

"Get away with you, you daft beggar!"

MRS. PATMORE

SEASON 3, EPISODE 9

RECIPE

SERVES:

INGREDIENTS

METHOD

"The more he said about how he liked his beef roasted and his eggs fried and his pancakes flipped, the more I wondered how to get away."

MRS. PATMORE

SEASON 3, EPISODE 9

RECIPE

SERVES:

INGREDIENTS

METHOD

"Would you mind taking the coffee up while it's still hot? Or is that too much to ask?"

MRS. PATMORE

SEASON 5, EPISODE 8

RECIPE

SERVES:

INGREDIENTS

METHOD

GEORGE

Can I lick the bowl?

MRS. PATMORE

Yes. You can both lick the bowl.

SEASON 6, EPISODE 1

RECIPE

SERVES:

INGREDIENTS

METHOD

"Well they've not turned out so badly, have they?"

MRS. PATMORE

SEASON 5, EPISODE 2

RECIPE

SERVES:

INGREDIENTS

METHOD

"I'd love to think I had a secret that was too indelicate for a lady's ear, but I haven't."

MRS. PATMORE

SEASON 5, EPISODE 5

RECIPE

SERVES:

INGREDIENTS

METHOD

"Oh, dear. We're not having another crisis, are we?"

MRS. PATMORE

SEASON 5, EPISODE 9

RECIPE

SERVES:

INGREDIENTS

METHOD

MOLESLEY

Can I borrow some soda, Mrs Patmore?

MRS. PATMORE

Borrow? So you'll give it back?

SEASON 6, EPISODE 2

RECIPE

SERVES:

INGREDIENTS

METHOD

"I'll crown you if you don't get that back on the heat."

MRS. PATMORE

SEASON 4, EPISODE 9

RECIPE

SERVES:

INGREDIENTS

METHOD

"We should celebrate. Come into the kitchen while I get the dinner going. There's a bottle of wine there and Mr. Carson wouldn't mind."

MRS. PATMORE

SEASON 6, EPISODE 7

RECIPE

SERVES:

INGREDIENTS

METHOD

"You're not a quick learner, are you?"

MRS. PATMORE

SEASON 6, EPISODE 2

RECIPE

SERVES:

INGREDIENTS

METHOD

DAISY

I can't believe Miss O'Brien would be so thoughtless.

MRS. PATMORE

Can't you? I can.

SEASON 4, EPISODE 1

RECIPE

SERVES:

INGREDIENTS

METHOD

"It never does good to hate anyone."

MRS. PATMORE

SEASON 6, EPISODE 4

RECIPE

SERVES:

INGREDIENTS

METHOD

"I'm crying because I don't want you to leave. I'll miss you. Don't, don't concern yourself. I'll get over it."

MRS. PATMORE

SEASON 5, EPISODE 8

RECIPE

SERVES:

INGREDIENTS

METHOD

"What the eye can't see,
the heart won't grieve over."

MRS. PATMORE

SEASON 1, EPISODE 5

RECIPE

SERVES:

INGREDIENTS

METHOD

MRS. PATMORE

Now spoon it into the shells.
No not like that! Oh, give it here!

DAISY

Mrs Patmore, we can do this.

MRS. PATMORE

Oh can you? With Ivy slapping
it out like a trained seal.

SEASON 4, EPISODE 3

RECIPE

SERVES:

INGREDIENTS

METHOD

"I cannot work from a new receipt at a moment's notice!"

MRS. PATMORE

SEASON 1, EPISODE 5

RECIPE

SERVES:

INGREDIENTS

METHOD

"Oh not those bowls, Ivy! Chilled soup should be an exquisite mouthful, not a bucket of slop!"

MRS. PATMORE

SEASON 4, EPISODE 3

NOTES

NOTES

NOTES

NOTES

NOTES

NOTES

NOTES

NOTES

INDEX
A — G

RECIPE	COURSE	PAGE

RECIPE	COURSE	PAGE

INDEX
N — S

RECIPE	COURSE	PAGE

INDEX
T — Z

RECIPE	COURSE	PAGE

KITCHEN MEASUREMENTS

CUP	TBSP	TSP	FL OZ
1/16 CUP	1 TBSP	3 TSP	½ FLOZ
⅛ CUP	2 TBSP	6 TSP	1 FLOZ
¼ CUP	4 TBSP	12 TSP	2 FLOZ
⅓ CUP	5⅓ TBSP	16 TSP	2⅔ FLOZ
½ CUP	8 TBSP	24 TSP	4 FLOZ
⅔ CUP	10⅔ TBSP	32 TSP	5⅓ FLOZ
¾ CUP	12 TBSP	36 TSP	6 FLOZ
1 CUP	16 TBSP	48 TSP	8 FLOZ

GALLON	QUART	PINT	CUP	FL OZ
1/16 GAL	¼ QT	½ PINTS	1 CUP	8 FLOZ
⅛ GAL	½ QT	1 PINTS	2 CUP	16 FLOZ
¼ GAL	1 QT	2 PINTS	4 CUP	32 FLOZ
½ GAL	2 QT	4 PINTS	8 CUP	64 FLOZ
1 GAL	4 QT	8 PINTS	16 CUP	128 FLOZ

WEIGHT

GRAMS	OUNCE
14 G	½ OZ
28 G	1 OZ
57 G	2 OZ
85 G	3 OZ
113 G	4 OZ
142 G	5 OZ
170 G	6 OZ
283 G	10 OZ
397 G	14 OZ
454 G	16 OZ
907 G	32 OZ

OVEN TEMPERATURES

CELSIUS	FAHRENHEIT
93°C	200°F
107°C	225°F
121°C	250°F
135°C	275°F
149°C	300°F
163°C	325°F
177°C	350°F
191°C	375°F
204°C	400°F
218°C	425°F
232°C	450°F

LENGTH

METRIC	2.5 CM	5 CM	10 CM	15 CM	20 CM	25 CM	30 CM
IMPERIAL	1 IN	2 IN	4 IN	6 IN	8 IN	10 IN	12 IN

Downton and Downton Abbey TM and © 2010-2021
Carnival Film & Television Limited.
All Rights Reserved.

weldon**owen**

Printed and bound in China
First published in 2021

10 9 8 7 6 5 4 3 2 1